Anika and the Magic Mat
A World of Mindfulness

By: Nora Gracie Foster

Illustrated by: Muddasir illustrations

Anika and the Magic Mat : A World of Mindfulness
Copyright © 2024 by Nora Gracie Foster - Home Time Art Press

All rights reserved. No part of this publication may be reproduced, distributed, or transmitted in any form or by any means, including photocopying, recording, or other electronic or mechanical methods, without the prior written permission of the publisher, except in the case of brief quotations embodied in critical reviews and certain other non-commercial uses permitted by copyright law.

Second Edition: 2024
Design and layout by Stefania Grieco
Published by Stefania Grieco
Hardcover ISBN: 978-1-7382735-7-7
Paperback ISBN: 978-1-7382735-6-0
E-book ISBN: 978-1-7382735-5-3

To the bright-eyed adventurers and dreamers of every corner of the playground,

This tale unfurls its pages for you! Just as Anika discovers the boundless wonders of a world stitched together with the threads of mindfulness, may you too find endless joy in the simple magic of being present.

May your days be woven with laughter, your steps guided by curiosity, and your moments filled with the rich tapestry of imagination.

In every breath, a new adventure awaits. In every stretch, a new story to tell. And in every heart, a space vast and deep as the sky for kindness, courage, and dreams.

Keep exploring, little yogis, for the world is a canvas, and you are the artists.

With a heart full of cheer and a mat rolled out in welcome,
Nora Gracie Foster and Your friends at
Home Time Art Press

Say hello to Anika, a pint-sized adventurer with a nose for knowledge and a room full of wild and woolly wonders.

Anika finds a yoga mat in her attic. Not just any mat, but one that looks like it could double as a magic carpet!

Whoosh! The mat glows like a disco ball and whisks Anika away to a forest so lush, even the trees seem to be holding their breath.

Anika strikes a pose with a wise owl who's so steady, he could be mistaken for a feathery branch.

Surf's up! Anika and a sea turtle twist into Cobra Pose, getting so bendy, they could tie themselves in knots.

City lights, cat's insights. Anika learns the Cat-Cow Pose, perfect for shaking off the city bustle.

Anika and a goat reach new heights with the Downward Dog Pose, stretching like they're trying to pull socks off with their toes

In the jungle boogie, Anika and a monkey swing into the Monkey Pose, ready to leap into the nearest banana tree.

The desert's no mirage as Anika and a camel arch into the Camel Pose, making shapes that would baffle a geometry teacher.

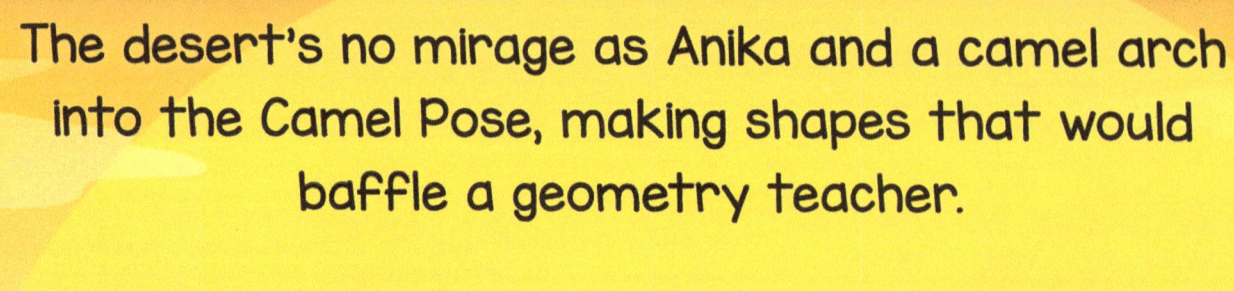

Dive deep! Anika and a fish practice the Fish Pose, blowing bubble rings like underwater champs.

Amidst the whispering bamboos, Anika and a panda sit so still in meditation, you'd think they were part of the furniture.

Chill out with a polar bear and Anika, mastering the Polar Breath that's cooler than a snow cone in winter.

Under a moonlit sky, Anika and a horse stand side by side, mastering the Horse Stance like midnight statues.

Eagle eyes on the prize! Anika and an eagle twist into the Eagle Pose with a view that could make birds jealous.

Anika chatters away with a parrot, learning a technique that could win them both a talk show.

Slow and steady wins the race as Anika and a tortoise bend into the Tortoise Pose, doubling as a perfect hiding spot.

Anika and a frog squat by the misty falls, ready to hop into the Frog Pose or a game of leapfrog.

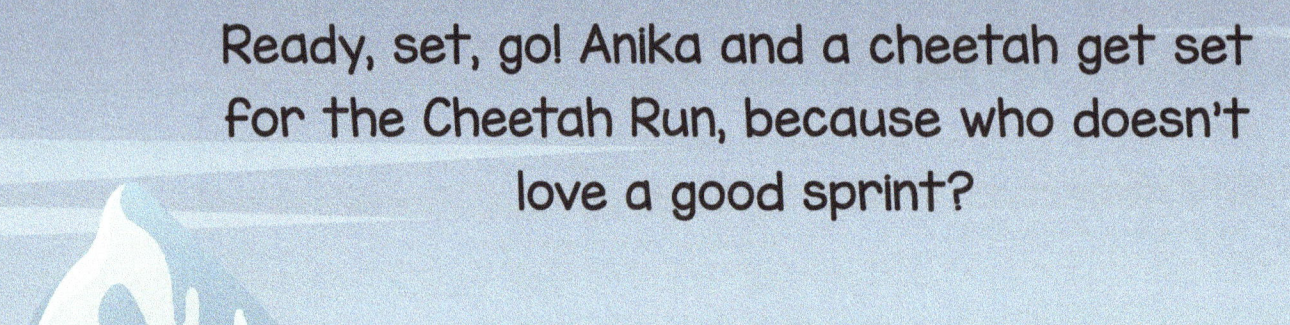

Ready, set, go! Anika and a cheetah get set for the Cheetah Run, because who doesn't love a good sprint?

Howling at the stars, Anika and a wolf meditate with a howl that might just be the universe's favorite tune.

Squirrel says, 'Jump!' and Anika leaps, mastering the Squirrel Jump with enough air to make a kangaroo clap.

Graceful as a swan, Anika glides across the pond, practicing the Swan Glide with a splendor that ducks could only dream of.

Dolphin dive into fun with Anika, where every splash is a laugh and every dive is a smile.

Up a sturdy oak tree, Anika follows an ant's climb, learning that perseverance can be a sticky situation.

With a dragon's fiery breath, Anika masters a technique that could toast marshmallows at twenty paces.

Flap into the Butterfly Flutter with Anika, where every beat is a giggle and the sky's the limit.

With the grace of a koi, Anika flows by the pond, making waves with the smooth moves of the Koi Flow.

Anika and a penguin slide into fun on a snowy hill that's slipperier than a banana peel at a comedy show.

High as an eagle, Anika learns the Soaring Meditation, floating on tranquility and a breeze of bliss.

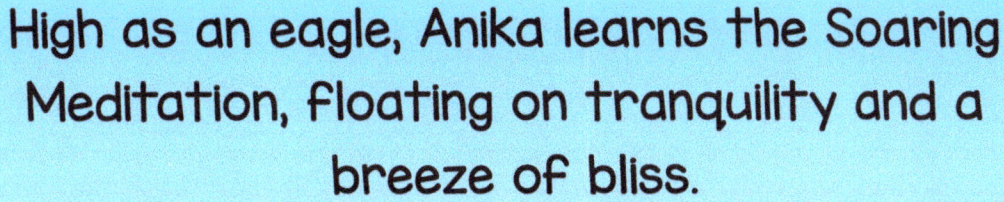

After a globe-trotting journey, Anika's heart is as full as a pizza on a Saturday night, with extra toppings of friendship and joy.

Back home, Anika's got tales to tell and poses to teach, turning her friends into mindful magicians on mats.

The End

Welcome to Anika's Activity Alcove, a place where fun and learning shine on every page! 🎨✨ If you're joining us on a tablet or want extra copies for more coloring and puzzle-solving fun, simply scan the QR code to download your very own activity book.

As you embark on this creative journey, we recommend using wax or pencil crayons for the activities. Markers might make a dash for it and bleed through, so let's keep the adventures tidy!

Here's a sneak peek at the fun ahead:

- Coloring Page: Warm up your crayons and add a splash of color to Anika's world.

- Sight Word Activity Page: Ready, set, read! Let's sharpen those word-spotting skills.

- Maze: Twist and turn through twists and turns with Anika

- **Shadow Pair Up:** Match the silhouettes in a game of playful shadows.

- **4x4 Grid Sudoku:** Place Anika and friends in a logic dance on the grid.

- **Word Search:** Seek out hidden words in a forest of letters.

- **Gratitude Tree Activity:** Reflect and draw what fills your heart with joy.

Once you've solved the puzzles, check the solutions to see how you did. And because we love to keep the fun going, the download includes a special journaling page to pen down your magical moments, plus a completion certificate to celebrate your achievements.

Grab your crayons and let's dive into a world of imagination and mindfulness with Anika and her enchanting friends! 🌳✏️

Happy exploring!

(WRITE WORD HERE)

Anika's Animal Adventure Sudoku

Place Anika, the dragon, turtle, and squirrel in the grid so each appears only once in every row and column. Solve the puzzle and help Anika's friends find their way home!

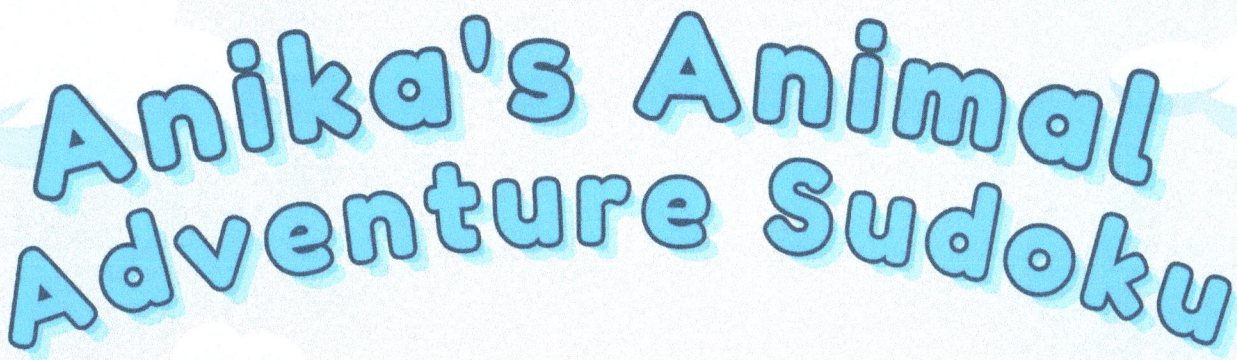

Anika's Mindful Word Quest

Search high and low across Anika's enchanted forest to find hidden words. Circle each one you discover!

```
            O T J
            Q F Q M
          L X K S Y S
          P J G Q L H
         W N U X M T A
           T A V L R
           T Y Y O W L
           U P
            R X
           Z L T V
           Y Z J L
          R F M Y U E
         G R A T I T U D E
       X F O R E S T M I N D F U L
       U E M A G I C P U I Y T A N
           L M Q R O F N
         B V L N Y H G N I R
         J N D L R H A A J K O
           R P Z         A X
                         N
```

ANIKA
MAGIC
TURTLE
FOREST
MINDFUL
YOGA
GRATITUDE
OWL

Anika's Gratitude Grove

Draw or write your joys on the leaves, feel their warmth, and if you're ever down, your Gratitude Tree will help turn your frown around!

Dear Super Explorer, 🌟

Hooray for you! 🎉 You've adventured through every page, solved every puzzle, and discovered the magic of mindfulness with Anika and her friends. Every step you took was a wonderful leap in learning and every challenge you conquered made you even more amazing!

Remember, the journey doesn't stop here. Just like Anika, you have so many more adventures waiting for you, each day, with new things to learn and explore. Keep being curious, keep being brave, and most of all, keep being the wonderful YOU.

We are all so proud of you! 👏

With lots of cheer,
Nora Gracie Foster
The Home Time Storytellers 📗

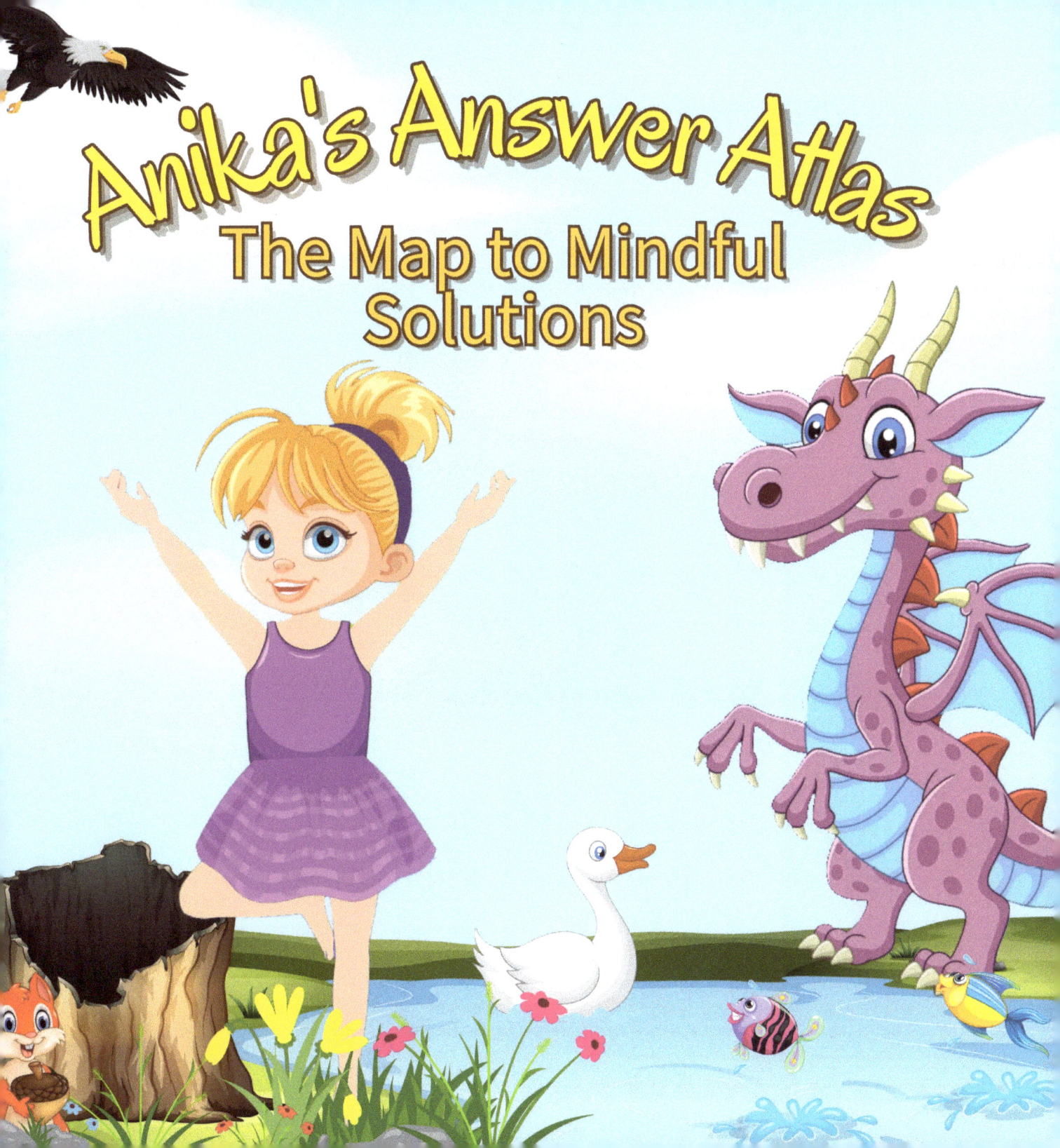

Anika's Animal Adventure Sudoku
Solution

Great job journeying through the puzzle. Here's how Anika and her animal friends found their perfect spots. Check your answers and see if you matched them just right!

Anika's Mindful Quest Unveiled

Great work, explorer! Here are all the hidden treasures you've found on your quest. Keep this magic for your next adventure!

```
        O T J
        Q F Q M
    L X K S Y S
    P J G Q L H
    W N U X M T A
      T A V L R
    T Y Y O W L
      T U P
        R X
      Z L T V
      Y Z J L
      R F M Y U E
    G R A T I T U D E
  X F O R E S T M I N D F U L
  U E M A G I C P U I Y T A N
        L M Q R O F N
      B V L N Y H G N I R
      J N D L R H A A J K O
        R P Z       A X
                    N
```

- ~~ANIKA~~
- ~~MAGIC~~
- ~~TURTLE~~
- ~~FOREST~~
- ~~MINDFUL~~
- ~~YOGA~~
- ~~GRATITUDE~~
- ~~OWL~~

Anika's Magical Mindfulness Moment

Instructions for Parents and Guardians:

This meditation is a gentle voyage into Anika's world, designed to help young minds unwind and connect with inner calm. Find a quiet, cozy space for your child to sit or lie down comfortably. Let's begin this serene adventure.

Anika's Enchanted Evening Guided Meditation

Take a slow breath in, feel your body relax, and as you exhale, let your day's adventures settle like the setting sun.

Imagine you're on Anika's magic mat, floating gently to a place where the sky blushes with dusky hues. Stars twinkle like little guides, leading you to a world of peace.

Beneath you, the mat lands beside a whispering river, its water softly glowing with the last light. You hear the sweet song of the night, inviting you to stretch out and gaze at the velvet sky.

Now, see the moon smiling down, bathing you in silvery light. The gentle night wraps around you like a soft blanket. With each breath, feel yourself sinking deeper into tranquility.

Anika's mat is your safe space, a magical corner of the world just for you. Breathe in the night's calm, breathe out all your worries. They drift away, leaving only quiet wonder.

When you're ready to return, wiggle your fingers and toes, bringing back the gentle energy of the night sky. Open your eyes to the world around you, carrying the quiet magic of Anika's evening with you.

About the Author

Nora Gracie Foster is a storyteller and artist who creates enchanting worlds for children aged 3 to 12. Her books are a fusion of imagination and learning, inviting young minds to embark on journeys filled with wonder and discovery. Drawing inspiration from the natural beauty of Canada and the rich cultural tapestry of Belize, Nora's stories are crafted to spark curiosity and instill a love of exploration.

Each book is an adventure that blends essential knowledge with playfulness, transforming reading into a delightful experience. Nora believes in the power of storytelling to educate and inspire, making every story an opportunity to teach and enchant.

With a passion for engaging young readers, Nora Gracie Foster continues to explore new horizons in children's literature. She invites her readers to join her on this magical journey, where education is not just a process but an unforgettable adventure.

About the Illustrator

Meet Pi, the creative heart behind Muddasir Illustrations. Hailing from Pakistan, Pi is a polyglot, fluent in English, German, Spanish, and Italian, enriching her illustrations with a global perspective.

Specializing in children's book and comic illustrations, Pi's art is a delightful fusion of vibrant colors and imaginative storytelling.

 Her tools range from traditional color pencils to modern Adobe Illustrator techniques. With over four years in the field, Pi, known as 'Kdpexpert' on Fiverr, crafts illustrations that resonate with the innocence and adventure of childhood. Her work not only captivates young minds but also inspires a lifelong love for reading. Through Muddasir Illustrations, Pi brings stories to life, creating magical experiences for children and adults alike. Join us in celebrating Pi's artistry, where each illustration is a journey into a world of wonder, joy, and endless possibilities.

Thank You for Joining Anika's Journey!

It's been a joy to share Anika's world of magic and mindfulness with you. We cherish your thoughts and would be delighted if you could spare a moment to leave a review.

Your insights not only brighten our path but also guide other families to join in the adventure of discovery, stretching imagination, and friendship.

Quick Review Links:

Please scan the QR code below to post your review on your preferred Amazon platform:

Amazon.com  Amazon.ca

If your magical mat landed elsewhere, we welcome reviews on any site you chose for your purchase.

With heartfelt thanks for your support, we eagerly anticipate our next enchanting tale together!

With gratitude and sparkle,
Nora Gracie Foster - The Home Time Storytellers
Creator of "Anika and the Magic Mat"

Magical Mantras
for Mini Yogis

Courage
I am brave, like Anika on her magical mat, ready for any adventure!

Peace
Peace flows within me, like a gentle river through a quiet forest.

Strength
My spirit is strong, standing tall like a mountain through wind and rain.

Gratitude
I cherish every moment, like a treasure found on an incredible journey.

Friendship
I am a friend to all, as welcoming as the shade of a spreading tree.

www.ingramcontent.com/pod-product-compliance
Lightning Source LLC
Chambersburg PA
CBHW042354070526
44585CB00028B/2927